JUBiLee

Readings
Through the Year

from

Alive Now

JUBILEE

Readings
Through the Year
from
Alive Now

UPPER ROOM BOOKS
NASHVILLE

Individual subscriptions to *Alive Now* are $11.95 per year. To order, contact *Alive Now*, P.O. Box 11239, Des Moines, IA 50340-1239; telephone: (800) 925-6847.

Cover and Interior Design: Susan Hulme
First Printing: September 1996 (5)

Library of Congress Cataloging-in-Publication

Jubilee : readings through the year from Alive now / edited by George R. Graham

      p.   cm.

   ISBN 0-8358-0786-X

   1. Devotional literature. I. Graham, George R., 1963-
  II. Alive now!
  BV4812.A1J82 1996
  242—dc20
96-5516
CIP
Printed in the United States of America

Acknowledgments: The art on pages 24, 42, and 120 is from *The Doré Bible Gallery*, illustrated by Gustave Doré and printed by the Henry Altemus Company; Philadelphia 1890. The art on pages 51, 55, and 56 is from *Blockprints for Sundays-Cycles A, B, C*, Copyright 1990 by The Order of St. Benedict, Inc. Published by The Liturgical Press, Collegeville, Minnesota. Used with permission. The art on pages 110 and 116 is from *Clip Art of the Christian World-Blocks for Sundays, Cycles A, B, C*, Copyright 1990 by The Order of St. Benedict, Inc. Published by The Liturgical Press, Collegeville, Minnesota. Used with permission.

*T*o the readers, writers,

photographers, artists, and staff,

past and present,

of *Alive Now* magazine.

Contents

Introduction

FOR A LONG TIME, I HAVE been fascinated with the concept of the Jubilee, which has its roots buried within the Holiness Code in Leviticus 25. In its direction once every fifty years to release captives, return property, forgive debts, and let the land and its inhabitants rest, this passage has always struck me as an unusual combination of law and prophetic vision. There is no evidence that the Jubilee was ever observed in ancient Israel, but strands of the tradition found their way into the Hebrew prophets and into the teachings of Jesus. When Jesus stands up in the synagogue at Nazareth, he reads words of Isaiah that promise good news to the poor, release to the captives, sight to the blind, and announce the year of God's favor (Luke 4:16-21). Jesus then declares that the scripture has been fulfilled in him. In a very

real way, Jesus proclaims the Jubilee in his life through his words and actions.

As followers of Christ, I believe we also are called to live out the Jubilee in our lives. Somehow we must find ways to announce the year of God's favor by offering good news to the poor, release to the captives, and healing to the sick. Not only is the tradition of Jubilee fascinating — it is also endlessly challenging! How do we begin to live out the Jubilee in our own lives? As I have struggled with this question, I have come to the conclusion that in order to grow in our ability to proclaim and live out the good news, we must continually seek to grow in our relationship with God. Growing in that relationship depends on our regularly seeking God through study, reflection, and prayer.

My hope is that this book

will not only help you proclaim the Jubilee to those around you, but that it will also offer regular support to you as you seek to grow closer to God. In each chapter you will find a focus scripture and an opening prayer, reflection questions, and suggested scripture readings, to enhance your use of the book as a resource to undergird your faith journey.

The organization of this book takes its cue from the church year, which provides a rhythm for the life of faith. Each chapter focuses on a different season of the church year, beginning with Advent, in which we keep watch for the coming of Christ to our world. Chapter Two on Christmas/ Epiphany helps us look at the implications of what Christ's coming means to us. Next is Lent, during which we repent of those things that separate us from God. Chapter Three focuses on the events of Holy Week, in which we follow Jesus from the triumphant entry into Jerusalem on Palm Sunday to his crucifixion on Good Friday. In Chapter Five, we look at the meaning of Easter in our lives. Chapter Six celebrates the birth of the Church at Pentecost. The final five chapters of the book are meant to illuminate issues of faith that might be considered during the expanse of time between Pentecost and Advent known as Ordinary Time. The topics for these chapters are Finding God in the Everyday, Living Faithfully, Seeking Community, Working for Justice, and Giving Thanks.

All of the readings in this book have appeared in *Alive Now* magazine, published by The Upper Room in Nashville, Tennessee. *Jubilee* was chosen as the title of this book not only because we as Christians are called to live out the Jubilee, but also because the publication of this book coincides with the silver anniversary of *Alive Now*. While in biblical terms it might be more appropriate to wait for our fifti-eth anniversary to celebrate a Jubilee, I believe that twenty-five years is a great milestone and certainly cause for celebration. As I looked back across the twenty-five years, the last four of which I have served as editor, proclaiming Jubilee seems to be at the heart of the mission of the magazine. I can think of no more fitting tribute to the magazine than to gather a collection of writing together under the title *Jubilee.*

In keeping with the tradition of *Alive Now,* this volume is the result of a group effort. I would like to thank JoAnn E. Miller for her encouraging response to the original proposal, Tom Page for the initial culling of material, Beth A. Richardson and Deen Thompson for invaluable help in finalizing content and preparing the manuscript, Karen F. Williams for overseeing the transformation from manuscript to book, and Susan Hulme for her superb design. I would also like to thank the writers, photographers, artists, and staff who have given life to the magazine for a quarter century. Without their work, this book would have been inconceivable.

As we selected pieces for the book, we have tried to capture a broad representation from across the years. If you are a regular reader of the magazine, we hope you find some of your favorite pieces within the pages of this book. If you have not been a regular reader, we hope this book introduces you to *Alive Now* and encourages you to consider forming an ongoing relationship with the magazine.

May this book become a faithful companion for you as you journey through the church year, growing closer to God and to the time when all in this world may experience Jubilee.

GEORGE R. GRAHAM
Martin Luther King Jr. Day

The days are surely coming, says the Lord, when I will fulfill the promise I made to the house of Israel and the house of Judah. In those days and at that time I will cause a righteous Branch to spring up for David; and he shall execute justice and righteousness in the land.

JEREMIAH 33:14-15

GOD OF THE ETERNAL PROMISE, IN A SEASON THAT IS FULL OF ACTIVITIES, HELP US QUIET OURSELVES AND KEEP WATCH FOR THE BIRTH OF THE ONE WHO IS OUR RIGHTEOUSNESS, JESUS CHRIST.

Amen

Waiting

ALL MY LIFE I HAVE WAITED: waited for the project to be completed, waited for supper to be ready, waited for the doctor to see me. I have waited at the traffic light, waited for the right relationship, waited to grow up.

I have waited alone or waited with friends. I have waited anxiously. I have waited expectantly. Some waits have brought joy. Other waits have brought bad news. Some waits have been "worth waiting for."

Now it is Advent, and I am waiting again. This time I am waiting in the darkness of my soul — ravaged by sorrow, anger, and fear. But I do not despair in the waiting, for I remember the way light looks and feels. The memories of silent nights with starlit skies are with me, and I have been bathed in the warmth of love's light. And so I hope — for the Messiah to come.

Voices sing, "Prepare him room." I know now waiting cannot be passive. There is something to do, but where? I have no inn or stable, but in my heart, I can make room. Move over doubt. Move over despair. Make room for Truth, for Life, for Love. Make room for the Prince of Peace.

KATHY CLARK-DICKENS

To Watch
for
Christ

To watch for Christ in the world is to see
that the spirit within us recognizes
the Spirit among us
so that spirit speaks to Spirit,
heart speaks to Heart,
love speaks to Love.

HENRI J. M. NOUWEN

Confessions of a Christmas Seeker

THE DECORATIONS HAD BEEN FEATURED prominently in stores for months. The pre-Christmas sales began as soon as the Halloween masks came down. The shelves had been stocked to overflowing. By the last few days before Christmas, though, they were beginning to empty. The very streets of the city proclaimed the coming holiday with larger than life candles and Santas lining the lamp posts and circling the courthouse. I searched among the clothes and toys and decorations, but in the midst of them all something was missing.

Soon wreaths began to appear on the doors of homes, and lights of many colors gleamed from windows, porches, and shrubs along the streets of town. Nativity scenes made of glass or pottery, wood or brass stood silently on coffee tables and in lighted cabinets. Mock forests of cut evergreens grew up overnight in parking lots. These thinned and, finally, disappeared as Christmas Day approached. I searched among the wreaths and lights and nativities and trees, but in the midst of them all something was missing.

Before long, Christmas cards began to season the mail in the box on the porch. At first, there were only a few; but as the days passed, more and more cards shared good wishes. Then came presents which shed their plain brown outer skins to reveal brightly colored packages. Soon the tree was dressed in lights and ornaments (many of which were gifts and reminded me of friends far away). I searched among the cards and gifts and thoughts of friends, but in the midst of them all something was missing.

Ah, and the parties! Dressed in the finest and most colorful clothes, wrapped in the latest fragrance, friends prepare to go. I turn to say, "The cedar makes the whole house smell good." We all agree, it does. The night is cold and the beautiful home in which the party is held radiates with the warmth of Christmas cheer. The food is good and the company is even better. This, surely, is what I have been searching for — what Christmas is really all about.

We are among the last to go, leaving behind the stacks of holiday plates and the crumpled paper balls we have made from our napkins. We walk out into the frigid dark of night. Still, I feel an empty place in my heart, aching to be filled. As my hand touches the icy handle of the car door, I hear something that seems to shatter the darkness like ice. It is the cry of a baby. Looking past the beautiful home in the side of the dark hills beyond, I see the faint light of a stable. I can see dimly the animals, and a man and woman bent over a manger looking into it as if it held the hope of all the world. Around them stand what looks to be people of the street — the homeless and hungry.

Suddenly, it came to me. I had been to the wrong party. Had I misread the invitation? Had I come to the wrong address? The

What are you looking for this Advent season?

What have you been missing during Advent?

Where have you found the Christ child this Advent season? Where else might you look?

party I had been seeking had taken place in a stable. Not a person I knew was there. Perhaps they were people I needed to know.

I went home and slept well that night. I had found the Christmas I had been looking for so long. And my wish for all of us is that we may each find that Christmas child as we pass through the wilderness of our world. I searched among the animals and the poor gathered in a stable to celebrate the birth of the child and in the midst of them all, there was nothing missing.

MICHAEL E. WILLIAMS

SUGGESTED SCRIPTURE READINGS:
Isaiah 11:1-10
Micah 5:2-5a
Matthew 3:1-12
Matthew 24:36-44
Luke 1:26-56

Blossom as a Rose

The wilderness of my soul cries out
So long a desert, desolate, barren, unyielding.
My spirit restless, weary, searching.
Come, Holy Child, foretold by prophets,
Blossom as a rose from roots of the eternal presence.
The parched land shall yield springs,
Water will flow freely,
Barren wastes become fruitful.
Come, Messianic Rose, illumine the caverns of my soul
With your purity, fragrance, freshness, beauty.
Transform and energize me as I drink
From refreshing streams in the desert.
Give strength to my hands, make firm my feet
As I leap and run with joy and singing.
I will rejoice forever in your glory and majesty.
Come, blossom as a rose, O Christ of Advent.

May Iwahashi

I NEED TO SING
SONGS OF
Christmas

I CAN HARDLY WAIT FOR Advent. I need to sing the songs of Christmas. My spirit longs to hear again the words of hope and peace. I wait for the smiles on faces to appear and to be greeted by strangers with words of joy and cheer. I want once more to feel the crush of crowds and (hopefully) see a snow-covered landscape.

Most of all, I want to be with family, as we worship together on Christmas Eve in a sanctuary that will have been made more beautiful with special decorations. The choirs will sing with fervor and the pastor will preach with eloquence, and we will sense the uniqueness of the moment. In a sense, history will repeat itself and Christ will be born anew. In homes, churches, and communities all across the world, for a few moments or a few days, we will see the human family at its best.

There will come a day, I pray, when the Christmas spirit will touch so deeply in the hearts of humankind that it will be sustained beyond a season so that the songs of Christmas will become the deeds of daily living.

WOODIE W. WHITE

Litanies for Advent and Christmas

by Beth A. Richardson

First Week of Advent

RESTORE

Reading: Psalm 80:1-7, 17-19

Litany

Today we enter Advent, a season of possibilities, a time of "not yet." But daily lives reflect human struggles. Sometimes we are surrounded by brokenness — in our lives, among our friends and families, in our worldwide family. Hope seems a far-off vision; yet we yearn for it to fill us. We cry together,

Restore us, O God; let your face shine, that we may be saved.

When hope is lost,

Restore us, O God.

When people are hurting,

Restore us, O God.

When nations are fighting,

Restore us, O God.

When children are hungry,

Restore us, O God.

Restore us, God of Life. Bring us closer to hope, the hope that lights the way on the journey to Bethlehem. During this season of waiting, may we be open to signs of your restoring love. As we light this first Advent candle, let us pray for God's restoration in the midst of brokenness and despair.

Restore us, O God; let your face shine, that we may be saved. Amen.

Suggested hymn: "O Come, O Come, Emmanuel"

Second Week of Advent
PREPARE
Reading: Mark 1:1-8

Litany
Listen to the voice of the one crying out in the wilderness:

Prepare the way of the Lord.

The time is coming, John the baptizer tells us. Now is the time to prepare for the coming of the Christ Child.

Prepare the way of the Lord.

Make the rough places smooth. Straighten the crooked places. Prepare all the paths so that hope may find its way.

Prepare the way of the Lord.

Make room for the Holy One. Empty out a space in the inn, in the stable, in the corners of our hearts. Make room in the busyness, in the crowds, in our filled-up, frantic lives.

Prepare the way of the Lord.

Heed the call to prepare space in our hearts and lives for Christ's birth. As we light this second candle of Advent, let us pray for wisdom and courage to prepare ourselves to receive God's Holy Child. Listen to the voice of the one crying out in the wilderness, Prepare the way.

Prepare the way of the Lord. Amen.

Suggested hymn: "Come, Thou Long Expected Jesus"

Third Week of Advent
PROCLAIM
Reading: Isaiah 61:1-4; 8-11

Litany
Rejoice greatly in the Lord. Proclaim God's greatness everywhere. For God loves justice and hates wrongdoing. God binds up the brokenhearted and comforts those who despair.

**I will greatly rejoice in the Lord,
my whole being shall exult in my God.**

Proclaim liberty to the captives and release to the prisoners. Proclaim comfort to those who mourn.

I will greatly rejoice in the Lord, my whole being shall exult in my God.

Proclaim the year of the Lord's favor, God's righteousness for the poor, the outcast, the vulnerable.

**I will greatly rejoice in the Lord,
my whole being shall exult in my God.**

Proclaim the coming of hope in a tiny baby, the birth of righteousness and peace for all nations.

**I will greatly rejoice in the Lord,
my whole being shall exult in my God.**

Spirit of God, anoint us as messengers of your good news to all people. As we light this third candle of Advent, let us proclaim the promised coming of God's righteousness through Jesus Christ.

**I will greatly rejoice in the Lord,
my whole being shall exult in my God. Amen.**

Suggested hymn: "Lift Up Your Heads, Ye Mighty Gates"

Fourth Week of Advent
RECEIVE
Reading: Luke 1:26-55

Litany
In this season of giving, we pause to open our hearts, our minds, our spirits to receive God's blessings. We proclaim with Mary,

My soul magnifies the Lord, and my spirit rejoices in God my Savior.

We have witnessed God's restoration in the midst of brokenness. We have prepared ourselves for Christ's coming. We have proclaimed with faith the promise of God's generous righteousness.

My soul magnifies the Lord, and my spirit rejoices in God my Savior.

Now we stand with welcome hearts, waiting to receive. Our spirits hunger for the coming of hope.

My soul magnifies the Lord, and my spirit rejoices in God my Savior.
Fill us, O God, with restoring love. Prepare us for the coming

of your Holy Child. Encourage us to proclaim the good news to all people.

My soul magnifies the Lord, and my spirit rejoices in God my Savior.

Like Mary, we are God's lowly servants. As we light this fourth candle of Advent, may we receive with Mary's openness and trust. Let us prepare to receive God's gift of hope.

My soul magnifies the Lord, and my spirit rejoices in God my Savior. Amen.

Suggested hymns: "Tell Out, My Soul"; "Lo, How a Rose E'er Blooming"

Christmas Day

REJOICE

Reading: Isaiah 52:7-10 and Luke 2:1-20

Litany
Christ Jesus comes to us this day. With the angels we sing, "Glory to God in the highest heaven!"

Together we sing for joy!

A baby has been born in Bethlehem. With the shepherds, we kneel before the manger of hope.

Together we sing for joy!

How beautiful upon the mountains are the feet of the messenger who announces peace, who brings good news, who announces salvation, who says to us, "Your God reigns."

Together we sing for joy!

Sing out with praise! Hope has come to us: to poor and rich, to old and young, to the infinite sky and the ravaged earth, to people of all nations and all hues of color.

Together we sing for joy!

Break forth together in singing! Jesus is born! As we light this candle, the candle which represents Christ, let us sing with praise and joy, for Hope is born today.

**Together we sing for joy! Jesus Christ is born!
Glory to God! Amen.**

Suggested hymn: "Joy to the World"

D*o not be afraid; for see — I am bringing you good news of great joy for all the people." . . . So [the shepherds] went with haste and found Mary and Joseph, and the child lying in the manger. When they saw this, they made known what had been told them about this child.*

LUKE 2:10, 16-17

GUSTAV DORÉ

GOD,

BORN INTO

OUR WORLD

AT CHRISTMAS,

HELP US RESPOND

TO THE GOOD NEWS

OF CHRIST'S BIRTH.

GIVE US COURAGE

TO LIVE

BEYOND OUR FEARS,

TO CHANGE

OUR LIVES,

AND TO TELL

THE GOOD NEWS

TO THE WORLD.

Amen

The *Christmas* Invitation

CONSIDER FOR A MOMENT those to whom the Christmas message came. A poor, bewildered carpenter and his young bride far from home; a group of cold and hungry shepherds; a worn-out innkeeper; and a trio of travel-weary wise old men. And throughout this holy infant's life it was with the hurting and the broken ones he chose to spend his time; and he was crucified among them at the end. So if you feel a little weary, a little rushed, a little breathless at the manger, then take heart because this message is for you.

Christmas speaks above all else to the poor and homeless, the hungry, oppressed, and friendless of our world. We must never let ourselves forget that, or our celebrations will be false as Santa's whiskers. But it also speaks to those who are burdened in any way, whether with regrets for the past, heartache in the present, or foreboding for the future. God says to us this night, "Be strong, fear not, for I am with you. I am for you and I will never let you go. Here is my son to prove it."

"What's the catch, then?" you may ask. "What about the fine print, the hidden costs, all those things I must give up in order to receive this gift, this love of God?" We're always looking for the catch in Christmas, always wary, fearful of what God will ask of us in return.

But suppose that God was truly and supremely and, above all else, the great Giver; just that, the great Giver. Just suppose that God, who devised this whole creation in the first place, knew all along that giving is really much more fun than getting. God knew that nothing in all creation can quite match the joy of seeing someone else unwrap a gift that you have chosen with your deepest and most careful love. That's what God is actually like, what God and love are really all about. So in giving us the Son, sending us the greatest gift there ever was or will be, God got such a charge, such a sheer delight out of the whole thing, that the entire creation laughed and rang with joy. That's what all the carols are telling us.

O come, all ye faithful, joyful and triumphant.

Join the triumph of the skies!

J. BARRIE SHEPHERD

Watch Your Step

Watch your step. You are approaching a dangerous manger.
It also serves as a makeshift baby bed.

Beware, for the one you seek did not stay a baby.

Jesus, nursed and cuddled by Mary, later claimed everyone who
does God's will as his mother.

Jesus, worshipped by shepherds, later challenged us to seek out not
lost sheep, but lost people.

Jesus, given gifts by wise ones who had traveled from afar,
called us to go out of our way to care for the hungry, the
lonely, and the homeless.

Watch your step as you take this Bethlehem baby into your
arms and whisper to him.

You may find him taking you into his arms, whispering new
life into you.

GEORGE WHITE

The Season
of Light

ON CHRISTMAS EVE following the cantata and communion service we drove to my home town. My brother was riding with us. As we entered town he said, "Drive through this neighborhood. There are supposed to be some houses around here decorated with luminaries."

So we did. And we were filled with wonder. Not just several, but dozens of houses were darkened, lit only by small candles in paper bags outlining the yards. Everywhere there was light – not a brilliant light by any means, but enough to break into the darkness, enough to see by, enough for hope, enough for surprising beauty.

So it is with my understanding of God's grace. My existence is illumined again and again by the showing forth of great love, not really largely or brilliantly; but in small ways, in gentle ways, in unexpectedly beautiful ways; with a word, a touch, a song, a story, a gift. And it is enough to live by.

SUSAN ROSS

*f*or Us

We try directing
the Christmas pageant
but the script is calling
for us to be onstage
for us to listen
for us to go with haste
for us to open the inn
for us to share the stable
for us to glimpse the star.

All the parts
have not been taken yet.

THOMAS JOHN CARLISLE

Finding Ourselves in the Story

JOSEPH WAS ONE OF those children who could completely disrupt a class in three seconds flat. No matter how well prepared the teacher, no matter how well planned our responses, Joseph could turn things upside down in a heartbeat. And on this particular day, Joseph was being especially challenging. We were trying to get ready for the Christmas play.

Joseph kept muttering, "Ain't coming to no Christmas play. I got better things to do! Wouldn't come if you gave me the best part! Hah!" We considered leaving him out altogether. In the end, I asked him to work with me. We would sit up front and help folks remember when to come and go. If the angels stayed a bit too long, we would prompt them to return to their seats.

"It's a really important part, Joseph. In fact, they can't do the play without us, so I hope you're going to be here."

"Told you I ain't got time for no stupid play. My mama's takin' me to the Christmas parade, and I'll be partying while all y'all in here fooling around." Joseph's mother worked two jobs, and it was not likely that she would take him to the Christmas parade.

Even so, we didn't expect to see Joseph that Sunday afternoon. But when I drove into the parking lot, 45 minutes early, there he was, all dressed up, sitting on the steps, waiting. One of the neighbors told me he'd been there for 30 minutes — just waiting. He greeted me with a smile and hug and was incredibly helpful. Joseph was willing to do whatever was asked of him and more. Made me wonder if this was the same child.

It was almost time for the play to start. Joseph was helping

⊸ What part do you play in the Jesus story?

⊸ What would be missing if you were not there? What can't be done without you?

⊸ What other parts are you being called to play?

⊸ What might it mean to invite everyone to find their place in the story?

SUGGESTED SCRIPTURE READINGS:

Isaiah 9:2-7

Isaiah 60:1-6

Matthew 1:18-25

Matthew 2:1-12

Luke 2:1-20

John 1:1-14

us get the younger children ready. One of the older boys came into the room, took one look at Joseph and hollered, "Thought you weren't comin' to no stupid play. Thought you had better things to do!"

I figured this was the end of the angelic behavior and waited for the explosion. Joseph turned to look at the older boy, then turned back to his work, declaring, "That was before I was in the story, stupid. See, now I'm in the story — they can't do it without me. Now I'm in the story — course I'm here."

What might it mean to invite persons to find their place in the story? To believe they are needed, they belong, and that we really can't live out this particular story unless they will come to be a part of it?

JANET WOLF

An Epiphany Litany

THE SEASON OF EPIPHANY begins January 6, celebrating the arrival of the Magi in Bethlehem to worship the child. It continues until the Transfiguration and the beginning of Lent. The word *Epiphany* means a showing forth or a revelation. During this time we get glimpses into who Jesus is. Even before we have asked the questions, God is revealing these truths to us — showing forth this Jesus as the Word Incarnate, the Giver of Life and Hope; offering us visible proof that in Jesus Christ the world's longing and liberation abide.

Look! Magi from the East watching the heavens to greet the Babe of Bethlehem.

Epiphany, the coming of dawn. Visible proof of the Bright Morning Star.

Look! Wise ones kneel in adoration — worshiping and offering their gifts.

Epiphany, an incarnation. Visible proof of the Promised One.

Look! A child in the temple proclaiming new hope.

Epiphany, a foretaste. Visible proof of the Word made Flesh.

Look! A baptism in the river Jordan. A voice declaring, "You are my beloved One."

Litany

Epiphany, a revelation. Visible proof of the Image of God.

Look! A wedding feast. Water turned into wine.

Epiphany, a showing forth. Visible proof of the Miracle Worker.

Look! Health restored: the blind, the lame, a servant and all who come.

Epiphany, a manifestation. Visible proof of the Great Physician.

Listen! Sins forgiven. "Who but God alone can do this?"

Epiphany, a realization. Visible proof of the True Liberator.

Listen! Parables told: the wheat and the tares, the mustard seed, hidden treasures. Stories of the Kingdom.

Epiphany, a demonstration. Visible proof of the Divine Teacher.

Listen! At the sound of a voice the wind is calmed, the sea stilled. "Why are you afraid?"

Epiphany, an assurance. Visible proof of the Mother's Wings.

Watch! On the mountain with Moses and Elijah. Face like the sun, clothes white as light.

Epiphany, a transfiguration. Visible proof of the Glorified One.

What we have seen, the world waits to see. What we have heard, the world waits to hear.

Come, Epiphany! Be visible in us today.

NORMAJEAN MATZKE

MERCIFUL GOD,
WITH OPEN ARMS
YOU INVITE ME BACK
TO YOUR EMBRACE
TIME AFTER TIME.
AS I EXAMINE
MY PRIORITIES
THIS LENTEN SEASON
HELP ME GROW
CLOSER TO YOU.

Amen

Yet even now, says the LORD, return to me with all your heart, with fasting, with weeping, and with mourning; rend your hearts and not your clothing. Return to the LORD, your God, [who] is gracious and merciful, slow to anger, and abounding in steadfast love, and relents from punishing.

JOEL 2:12-13

From Dust You Came

ALTHOUGH ASH WEDNESDAY is not an obligatory observance on the church calendar, churches are habitually filled on this day. There is something about the gesture of marking with ashes the sign of the cross on one's forehead that captures the religious imagination. It is a gesture that explicitly calls to mind our mortality. "Remember you are human" or "From dust you came, to dust you will return" are the words that traditionally accompany the signing of the cross that leaves that unmistakable black smudge on one's forehead. The thought is sobering but not morbid. For the truth is that considering the larger scheme of things we live only a very short time. And the reminder of that reality can serve to put our present situation into clear perspective. . . .

Ash Wednesday is such a diagnostic moment for all of us. The ritual is strikingly simple and ruthlessly egalitarian. None of us is excused from the procession. The smudgy mark does not adhere differently to man or woman, wealthy or destitute, educated or ignorant, compassionate or cruel. It labels us as one of the species, one of the mortals, who like everything else in this created universe, will lose its present form. We will die. This is a certainty we share with each other. . . . We would

Three REFLECTION

Lent is a time for identifying and letting go of the things that block your relationship with God. Use the following questions daily or weekly as a part of your Lenten reflections:

☞ *What has kept you from engaging God?*

☞ *What has made you feel distant and alienated from the Divine One?*

☞ *After you have considered these questions, reflect on whether there is something you could give up or take up during Lent that would help you grow closer to God.*

Suggested Scripture Readings:

Joel 2:1-2, 12-17

Psalm 51:1-17

Isaiah 55:1-9

Matthew 4:1-11

Mark 8:31-38

John 2:13-22

1 Corinthians 1:18-25

like to live in ultimate control. We would prefer to be able to predict our futures and sketch our own life designs. But, in truth, we are merely collaborators in a larger design which is neither entirely under our control nor of our individual making.

By this, I do not mean to suggest that we should lead willy-nilly lives, buffeted about by every changing fad and circumstance. We do need to be intentional in our choices. We do need discipline, rhythm, and design to shape our work, our worship, and our relationships. What I am referring to is an ultimately very deep and existential trust in the process of life itself, a trust in the providence of God. . . .

The gesture of the imposition of ashes is an invitation . . . to change and to grow, and in the process to die to the narrowness and limitations of the familiar selves of our present making.

WENDY M. WRIGHT
The Rising

Lenten
Confession

We come before you, Renewing Spirit, like trees
scarred from the harshness of winter's ice which has
overwhelmed us, encased us, broken us, shattered
our illusions of ourselves.

We confess we have not yet let go of the pain or
pruned away the scars. Shatter our illusions of ourselves, O God. Let them fall away like ice breaking
loose in the sun's warmth. Let them shatter down
like glass breaking. Let the noise awaken
us from our slumbers.

And, as spring brings its strongest signs of new
growth to the limbs scarred by winter, so let
our scars become sources of love to your
other scarred and wounded children.
Amen.

DWIGHT H. JUDY

A Poem of Preparation

Somewhere
> between the ground hog and the March lion
>> near the Valentine gifts
> and the birthdays of Presidents,
>> in the expanding days
>>> of shrinking snowdrifts,
>> before the icicles last drop,
>>> and the daffodils first thrust,

Somewhere
> between snowscape and wheatscape,
>> out of the silence of winter,
>>> and into the bird-loud spring,
> comes a season we too often decide
>> to forget.
> Between Fat Tuesday and Good Friday,
>> the growing light casts
>>> a lengthening shadow,
>> as ashes prepare us for
>>> blood and fire,
>> that will melt our stony hearts
>>> into a waiting tomb.

Could this holy season
> be like others we have known?
Shall we go up again to Jerusalem,
> the killer of prophets?
Will we journey with one who can
> call down fire from heaven,
>> but would rather have our tears?
Might the palm branch flourish,

or wither to a cross?
Can this easy yoke be
    fashioned from a tree?
Can a thorny crown utter silent truth
    to this arrogant world?
Will we follow this courage that
    ripens toward a borrowed grave?

Somewhere
    between pause and preparation,
        promise and fulfillment,
Lent is the season of the journey,
        and the journey of this season;
        a springtime that blossoms red,
        grows thorns and nails,
        turns followers into fools,
        and breaks all our bones of pride.
    Rendering us
        beyond all pleading between two thieves,
        beyond all wonder, between the dark noon
        and the blazing midnight,
        and beyond all expectation
        for the absolutely absurd.
    Astonishment of Easter,
        when myrrh turns into music,
        doubt's denial into faith's glad boast,
    And all the granite cracks and breaks
        before loud lilies trumpeting to the sun.

GRAHAM OWEN HUTCHINS

No Shortcuts

Can I find my way into Easter morning without contemplating the life and passion of the Savior? It seems that I try. But I soon learn there are no shortcuts to the sunrise.

Jesus took no shortcuts to the empty tomb.

My spirit is hungry to know wholeness. But first I must let God speak and tell me what is broken.

For Jesus took no shortcuts to the empty tomb.

In quiet contemplation, God's spirit begins to reveal the inner recesses of my soul:

my insecurity and fear of not being accepted,
my subtle anger and unreconciled relationships,
my need to achieve and my unrealistic expectations
of myself and others,
my lack of inner solitude and my need for busyness.

But Jesus says to me, "For those things I died."

And Jesus took no shortcuts to the empty tomb.

Slowly, I come to know that I find my way to Easter morning as I work my way through the maze of unforgiven sin within my own spirit. It hurts sometimes, that inward looking. But I can see Easter on the horizon.

And then I know, Jesus took no shortcuts to the empty tomb.

LYNN BROOKSHIRE

Call forth Life

Read John 11:1-44

When all my hopes and dreams
lie in the dust,

And possibility is bound
in lazarus-graveclothes;

When my bethany-road
is strewn with martha-bitterness
and mary-regrets;

Come, Lord,
come with hope-filled gait,
swirling the road dust
with sandled feet,

And seeing the future,
even through tear-filled eyes,
Call forth life once more.

ROBIN E. VAN CLEEF

T*hen [Jesus] took the twelve aside and said to them, "See, we are going up to Jerusalem, and everything that is written about the Son of Man by the prophets will be accomplished."*

LUKE 18:31

FAITHFUL CHRIST, AS YOU MAKE YOUR WAY TO THE CROSS — SUFFERING, CRUCIFIED, DYING — HELP ME FOLLOW IN THE WAY OF YOUR REMARKABLE FAITH.

Amen

GUSTAV DORÉ

It Is Palm Sunday

Passion-full.
The cardinal outside my window
sings his heart out brightly
(almost like music for the journey,
almost like song to welcome king).

The sky above offers misty gray,
and in the far distance
church bells ring out,
calling people to praise with palm.

I try to set my eyes and heart
toward Jerusalem as Jesus did.
My hands can barely raise the palm
though I long to call him Lord
and yearn to sing him as King.

It's the thought of Thursday coming
and the sadness mixed with bread.
It's the thought of Friday coming
and my voice among the rabble.

It is Palm Sunday. Passion-full.
You pass before me, Lord Jesus,
and your eyes meet mine in greeting.
I cannot bear to keep on looking,
for you have seen into my soul.

It is Palm Sunday, Lord and King,
and I am helpless, sinful here before you.
Only strength and grace from you
will courage me to walk with you,
to raise my palm in greeting,
to walk along with you in journey,
this long and painful week.

Only open hands before you
will allow me entrance into Jerusalem.
Only knowledge of your great compassion
will let me stand before your cross.

It is Palm Sunday, Jesus-Savior;
now I raise my waving palm
and greet you again as you pass,
knowing you know, knowing you love,
and that you will be waiting for me
near the tomb on Easter morn.

JOYCE RUPP, OSM

A Visible Reminder of Love
Maundy Thursday Meditation

WHEN I WAS 13 and invincible, the last thing I wanted was anything which tied me to my mother and said in some way, "You still need my love and protection!" But my mother knew better, having seen much more clearly just what the world throws at a person. So she gave me two things. "Just to help you remember I love you," she said. One was a name bracelet; the other was a pocket New Testament. I carried them through Vietnam. Or maybe they carried me; I am no longer certain.

Until recently when the clasp broke, I wore the bracelet — a visible reminder of love when the road got dark and the wind got strong. The mud-caked New Testament now sits in my office where others need to hear that someone still loves them, even when the world seems too wild for safety.

When the first meal of Communion was held, the disciples also thought they were invincible . . . or at least they were convinced Jesus was. They were young men who probably recoiled at the thought that they would need another's love and protection. But Jesus knew better. He had a much deeper comprehension of the evil that could — and would — engulf even the most faithful of followers. So he gave them two things. "Just to keep you safe and assure you of my love while you remain in the world," he said gently. One was his name; the other was a meal.

We like to believe that as faithful followers we have carried his name all over the world. But I think that perhaps it's the Name that has carried us all over the world. The bread and cup have nurtured us through two millennia — visible reminders of love when the road gets dark and the wind gets strong.

Like those gifts from my mother, the bread and cup are intended to accompany us into places of pain and danger. Sometimes the bread has been prisoner's hardtack and the cup a brief swallow by a hospital bed. Jesus never asked that we be exempted from the world's desolation. Indeed his name seems to draw oppression toward us.

But he did promise to be with us, even amid the anguish of the soul. So as we join together tonight in the meal, let us receive what is being offered: a visible reminder of Christ's love . . . to carry with us when the road gets dark and the wind gets strong. Shalom!

DONALD D. DENTON, JR.

The *Crown* Maker

THE TASK SEEMED simple enough. We needed a crown of thorns to put on the altar in church during Lent. Since I live in blackberry country, I was glad to volunteer to make one.

On a cool, crisp February morning I buttoned my coat, gathered my pruning clippers and gloves and headed off down the gravel road. It wasn't long before I had tied my jacket around my waist and was caught up in the birds singing and the wind rustling through the trees.

I trudged down a bank to the blackberry patch. There I discovered that not just any vine would do. In order to bend without breaking, the vines could neither be too green nor too dry. The best vines would also produce thorns that were long and strong. I found several and began clipping. I wondered if this were how it had been done 2,000 years ago — thorn bush cuttings made along the road amidst sounds of congenial chatter and fast-approaching spring.

Soon I had my materials and began to head home. The afternoon sky was now darkening and I pulled my jacket tightly around me.

On the driveway I spread out my wares: various lengths and thicknesses of blackberry vines all with equally pointed thorns, and a few pieces of wire.

As I began to bend and plait the branches, I discovered the gloves were of no use. They only got caught on the thorns and stuck to them. If I was going to make this crown of thorns, I was going to have to do it bare-handed.

After a few twists, my fingers were punctured and bleeding. I stopped and looked at my hands. The person who fashioned the crown for Christ could not have done so without some injury,

≪≫ *When have you denied or disappointed Jesus?*

≪≫ *What was the situation?*

≪≫ *What were your thoughts? feelings?*

≪≫ *What contributed to your actions of denial?*

≪≫ *Can you think of one concrete action you could take during Holy Week that would be an affirmation, rather than a denial, of Jesus?*

SUGGESTED SCRIPTURE READINGS:

Psalm 31:9-16
Isaiah 53:4-9
Mark 11:1-11
Luke 22:14-23:56
John 13:1-17, 31b-55
1 Corinthians 11:23-26

some pain to himself.

Slowly I continued to wrap. As I did, I was making that crown for my Lord all over again. He was here. The crown was real. Tears mixed with the blood from my fingers while I completed the task.

I secured the last piece of wire and stepped back to look at my creation. Nursing my throbbing fingers, I wondered about that first crown maker.

Had he, too, been surprised by his own pain and wondered about the pain he was causing this man named Jesus? Had he sensed something timeless about that act of weaving a circle of thorns? Had he felt my fingers next to his? And when he saw that Man hanging on the cross wearing the crown he had made, did he know he had already been forgiven?

The plop, plop of early spring drops splattered on the pavement. I held out my hands to the cooling, soothing rain, thankful for the forgiveness that comes to all crown makers.

NORMAJEAN MATZKE

To a Man on a Cross

Jesus,
I know this isn't the time,
but it's important for me to know
before you go:
    Would you do it again?
    Knowing what you now know,
    would you start all over
        from cradle
        to cross?
Is the present pain
    worth the future promise?
Is the heaven of life
    worth the hell of death?

I get so frightened, Lord!
Too scared to live,
too scared to die.
I don't understand life,
it gets so muddled in my mind:
    evil and good,
    birth and death,

    suffering and salvation.
Why are they so difficult
    to distinguish?
The unknown frightens me.

I have no faith
that Fridays are not final.
And yet,
and yet,
I cannot quite abandon hope.
Is it only from this hill
that you can see the sunrise?

Jesus,
    if you must go,
    then come again
    and raise me up
    so that your Easter
    means my resurrection, too.

J. Bradley McNaught

MONOLOGUE FOR ANY
Friday

Unlike those who crucify
or lynch or shoot and leave to die,
my sin is that of standing by.
It's true I would not do the deed.
My life seems marked by love, not greed.
And yet I carry deep the seed
of guilt because of my consent.
I know full well just what is meant
by prejudice. I might have lent
my strength in protest to the acts
of which I disapprove. The fact
that they occur and reoccur attracts
my notice, not my plan of life.
I'd stamp out all dissension and all strife,
but, God, I'd rather die than give my life.

MURIEL THIESSEN STACKLEY

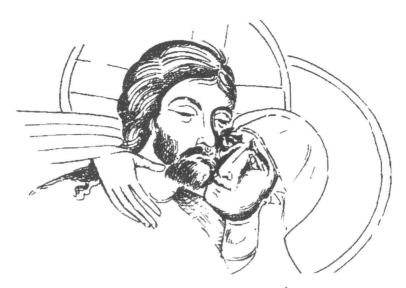

Holy Saturday

You were a deep and
Vital dream
Now you lie
Broken
Shattered
Dead
Entombed

I walk away from you
Along a dry and dusty road
Yearning
For someone
To interpret the Scriptures
For my heart to burn within
Desperately hoping this road
Leads to Emmaus

Susan W. N. Ruach

Holy Week
Prayers

BY BETH A. RICHARDSON

Passion Sunday

Hosanna! Blessed is the one who comes in the name of the Lord.

Today we enter Holy Week, with its cycle of life, death, and new life.

Hosanna! Blessed is the one who comes in the name of the Lord.

Jesus, the holy one, the whole one, enters Jerusalem as he rides on the back of a donkey colt. Crowds wave palm branches and cry out,

Hosanna! Blessed is the one who comes in the name of the Lord.

Jesus, holy one, enter the gates of our hearts today as we join you in this time of your Passion. With you, let us remember and celebrate your birth, your calling, your ministry.

Hosanna! Blessed is the one who comes in the name of the Lord.

Jesus, our mentor of wholeness, guide us through the streets of our journey. Open our eyes and our ears to the guiding of God's spirit who calls us to costly faithfulness and to joyous wholeness. Let us sing with all our selves,

Hosanna! Blessed is the one who comes in the name of the Lord.
Hosanna in the highest heaven. Amen.

Holy Thursday

One of you will betray me.

Surely not I, Lord? Broken promises, broken relationships, broken dreams. Surely not I, Lord?

This is my body, which is given for you. Do this in remembrance of me.

Jesus' body broken. The whole one is broken, and out of that fracture come reclaimed dreams and spirit.

This cup that is poured out for you is the new covenant in my blood.

Jesus' blood shed. The holy one is wounded, and out of that wound come new promises and life.

The words I have spoken to you are spirit and life.

Jesus calls to us through our blindness and confusion, our woundedness and our fear, to follow him into the unknown. To sit with him while he prays. To go with him through hurt and humiliation. To trust that the journey is bearable because Jesus is traveling before us and with us.

The words I have spoken to you are spirit and life.
Come, follow me. Amen.

Good Friday

When they came to the place that is called The Skull, they crucified Jesus there with the criminals, one on his right and one on his left.

Jesus, the holy one, was ridiculed, tortured, and hung on a cross to die. And Jesus said, "Father, forgive them; for they do not know what they are doing."

The leaders scoffed at him, saying, "He saved others; let him save himself if he is the Messiah of God, his chosen one."

We stand by, helplessly, watching our Hope of hopes die his slow death.

Darkness came over the whole land until three in the afternoon, while the sun's light failed; and the curtain of the temple was torn in two. Then Jesus, crying with a loud voice, said, "Father, into your hands I commend my spirit." Having said this, he breathed his last.

We call to you, God, from this dark, lifeless place. Do not leave us here. We hurt deeply. We sink low in sadness. We reach up to you with pleading hands. Hold on to us, O God. Let us hear your voice of hope and see your light of healing.

I am the resurrection and the life. Those who believe in me, even though they die, will live, and everyone who lives and believes in me will never die. Amen.

The angel said to the women, "Do not be afraid; I know that you are looking for Jesus who was crucified. He is not here; for he has been raised, as he said."

MATTHEW 28:5-6

SAVIOR OF THE RESURRECTION, THE EMPTY TOMB SHOWS YOU BRING LIFE FROM DEATH, HOPE FROM DESPAIR. DISSOLVE OUR WORRIES, GRANT US WHOLENESS, GIVE US EASTER FAITH. IN THE NAME OF THE RISEN SAVIOR, ALLELUIA!

Amen

The Day before Easter

I AM MARRIED. I am the mother of three children. I am the pastor of a congregation. Each day is a challenge. Each day brings its own rewards. Each day I rely on God to get me through. This was especially true one day last year — the Saturday before Easter. The week had already been full with Palm Sunday, Maundy Thursday, and Good Friday services.

In addition, I had been called upon to minister to a young family who had just experienced the loss of twin daughters. The babies had been taken prematurely in order to save the mother's life. The mother was still in the hospital. I met with the family on Thursday to plan the funeral service, scheduled for Saturday afternoon. Saturday morning I got up real early to get my thoughts in order for the funeral. This was my very first funeral for children. What could I say to grieving parents on the day before Easter? Would the message of resurrection be something they could hear or accept? I struggled with my words. Nothing seemed quite right. I knew I would have to speak from my heart.

As I worked, my middle child, eight-year-old Alex, came downstairs. "Why are you up so early?" I asked. "Can't you go back to bed? Mommy needs to get some work done." "I don't feel good," he answered. "The top of my head hurts." I looked him over — and there they were — bright red spots on his face, his stomach, and the top of his head. Chicken pox! I couldn't believe it. Chicken pox! On the day before Easter! I didn't know whether to laugh or cry. What now! Besides the funeral that afternoon, there were other things I had planned on getting done: coloring eggs with the children and an Easter egg hunt with friends down the street; I had new Easter outfits to hem and three Easter baskets to fill. The time changed that night and we would all lose an hour's sleep. We needed to be at church by 6:30 the next morning for the sunrise service. Who would watch Alex? Would the other children get sick, too? My head was spinning. How in the world would I get through this day and feel at all like celebrating on Easter morning?

Well, somehow everything did get done. At the funeral I spoke as bravely as I could. With tears in my eyes I proclaimed God's suffering love to that mother and father and brother. I will never forget seeing those tiny baby girls lying together in their tiny white casket. I will never forget driving to the cemetery with the funeral director and the parents. The mother held the casket on her lap. My heart was filled with emotion for this family.

At the same time I was concerned about my own son at home who wasn't feeling well and who needed me. I spent the rest of the day doing those other mothering things. I went to bed late that night feeling physically and emotionally exhausted.

But when the sun rose on Easter morning, my heart and spirit rejoiced. I went to church ready to celebrate the resurrection. I sang the alleluias with tears in my eyes as I remembered the babies I had buried the day before. But this was indeed the day of resurrection. And God is indeed the God who gives life to the dead, and strength to the weary, and hope to all those who need hope. Even me. On Easter Day. And every day.

God gives me what I need. That's what I have learned over these years of trying to balance pastoring and parenting, work and home. Seldom do I feel adequate to do what I am called to do. Hardly any day goes as I have planned or intended it. Crises are the norm rather than the exception. But I try to keep open to God's leading and direction. For the most part, life is good. With laughter and tears, with hopes and prayers, with help from family and friends, I go forward in faith. God is with me. I am not alone.

KAREN BURTNER GRAHAM

God's Garden

Out of the ruins, a lily;
    out of the desert, a rose;
        signs of life in the midst of death.

Form rises out of chaos.
    Color emerges from lifeless grey,
        and cross-nails become lily stems
            opening out into gleaming white bells.

Horror is transmuted into beauty,
    pain into fragrance,
        despair into hope,
            death into life.

Thus it was.
    Thus it is now.
        Thus it will ever be.

Christ is risen!
    Alleluia!

ROBIN E. VAN CLEEF

Mary Magdalene

on the first day of the week

The night drags on and on.
My prayers bounce back like boomerangs.
It's now three days
Since Jesus died in agony.

Before day comes, I stumble out the door,
To anywhere at all that isn't here.
With dew-soaked feet, I watch dawn fingerpaint
Rose streaks and orange-red across the sky.

Nothing has changed.
The sun rose yesterday; it will tomorrow.
My morning walk will end up at a tomb,
Another hopeless hassle with a stone
I know already that I'll never budge alone.

But atoms in my body lilt with life.
Though I well know the grief ahead, I run.
And suddenly, incredulous, I find
That stone, the one I couldn't budge,
Is rolled away.

KIT KUPERSTOCK

Read John 20:1-18

Imagine that you are Mary Magdalene and that you have gone to Jesus' tomb early on the third day.

⇨ *When you see the stone rolled away, what do you think? feel?*

As you stand by the tomb distraught because Jesus is not there, people ask why you are weeping. Finally you hear the familiar voice of Jesus call you by name. How do you respond?

⇨ *Jesus asks you to tell the others you have seen him. Where do you go? How do you tell them? How do they respond?*

SUGGESTED
SCRIPTURE
READINGS:

Psalm 118:1-2, 14-24

Matthew 28:1-10

Luke 24:13-35

John 20:24-31

John 21

1 Corinthians 15:1-11

The One Who Walks Through *Walls*

The disciples huddled behind locked doors,
    hearts numbed by grief
        eyes swollen with sadness
            hearts broken by Jesus' death.

Then the Risen Christ
    jolted them awake from grief's nightmare.
        He walked right through their fear-etched walls.

The Risen Christ is still surprising us,
    walking through the walls we build,
        entering places forbidden to him,
            coming to us in our self-imposed
                prisons of doubt and fear.

May the Risen Christ who walks through walls
    enter that part of your life
        which you have walled off with fear.

GEORGE WHITE

The Wonderful News

THE WONDERFUL NEWS OF resurrection shouts that Christ is here! He is still in our presence. Even though we are hard pressed to live consistently as believers, we can find strength and hope in the face of Jesus.

Jesus is present. His promise to never leave or forsake us is still good, but where should we look?

Our quest leads us to find him in the obvious and in the unlikely, in the comforter and the stranger, in the beautiful and the unbeautiful. His presence resides in that which is dangerous as well as in safety, in enemies as well as in our friends, in those who speak the same things and those who have other ideas. In both the successful and the defeated, the wealthy and the poor, Jesus can be found. Jesus is present when the table is empty and when there is bread and wine. That promise of presence has no limitations.

Following Christ means not only celebrating the good news but living it. With responsibility, courage, and vision, we can open ourselves to that loving presence wherever Christ appears.

PAMELA J. CROSBY

My Resurrection

I cannot bring myself
to choose to carry
a crossbeamed burden
or to welcome nails
in order to merit
(if merit is the word)
an Easter of my own.

And yet
and yet
I cannot quite
abandon
the hope of Easter.

If I believed it
I would run
like John
and Peter
through the morning.

I would dance
like Mary Magdalene
in the garden
of her second spring
the gavotte
of sudden surprise
and suddener certainty
his second coming
to her.

I would exclaim
like Thomas
when I recognized
the telltale wounds
which guaranteed
the passion
of the person
he confronted —
the presence

of a friend
much more than friend.

But still
like Peter
I would need to answer
the pertinent
recurrent question
Do you love me?
and not by words
alone.

And yet
I do.
I do.
I do.

Lord, overlook
the insouciance
the impotence
the arrogance
of my undoing
and my abstinence
from love
and loving-kindness.

Raise me up
so that your Easter
means my resurrection too.

Fulfill your promise
I am with you always.

THOMAS JOHN CARLISLE

All of them were filled with the Holy Spirit and began to speak in other languages, as the Spirit gave them ability.

ACTS 2:4

GOD

OF PENTECOST,

OPEN OUR HEARTS

TO RECEIVE

THE DIVERSE GIFTS

OF THE SPIRIT.

HELP US USE

THESE GIFTS

TO SPEAK

THE GOOD NEWS

TO THE NEEDS

OF THIS WORLD.

NICK LONG

Languages of Faith

WHEN I WAS IN COLLEGE, I worshiped in a small community church. On Pentecost, the pastor invited members of the congregation to speak words of greeting in as many languages as possible. We usually counted more than a dozen, which was not bad for a congregation fewer than a hundred.

In some small way, our efforts in pidgin French and faltering Swahili gave us a sense of what the apostles must have felt on that first Pentecost when they found themselves filled with the Holy Spirit and able to speak in all the languages of those gathered.

While this ability to speak the languages of the people gathered was an important sign, the significance of Pentecost was much deeper. The account of Pentecost in Acts 2 shows the depth of God's commitment to us. Not only did God send Jesus Christ to redeem us. God sent the Holy Spirit to bring us gifts and to sustain us.

Pentecost also marks the birth of the Church. I am amazed at how quickly Acts 2 moves from God's gift of the Holy Spirit to the apostles' response of doing the work of the Church. Upon receiving the Holy Spirit, the apostles left the closed room where they had been meeting. Immediately they began to spread the good news. Peter called the gathered people to commitment, and many responded. The apostles and the newly

⇨ What particular language of faith has the Holy Spirit given you? What gifts has God given you that you can use to spread the good news?

⇨ To whom are you called to speak?

⇨ What might you say or do to witness to God's commitment to them?

SUGGESTED SCRIPTURE READINGS:

Psalm 104:24-34
John 14:8-17, 25-27
Acts 2:1-21
1 Corinthians 12:4-11

baptized lived in response to God's commitment to them through Christ and the Holy Spirit.

Acts is one of the most aptly named books of the Bible. The apostles express their faith by preaching, teaching, and healing. They challenge us to spread the good news in a world that desperately needs it. The apostles' actions provide a model for our life in the Church. We are called to hear the call to commitment to the gospel and to go out in committed service.

In the two millennia since the first Pentecost, the challenge of living a committed life has not decreased, but neither has God's commitment. Just like the apostles, the Holy Spirit gives each of us a particular language of faith to speak. May we speak that language to a world that needs to hear much more about God's commitment to it.

GEORGE R. GRAHAM

Pentecost Prayer

God above all other gods,
    giver of life and new life:

Today we celebrate
    the coming of your Holy Spirit
    and the birth of the church.

But we seek more than memory, Holy One.
    We seek the reality
    of our own Pentecost
    this very day.

Perhaps tongues of fire and a mighty wind
    are too much to expect.
    Yet we ask that your presence
    flame in our hearts today
    and transform our lives,

Just as you flamed in the disciples' hearts
    and transformed their lives
    so long ago.

Birth again your church this day
    by the living fire of your Spirit.
Amen.

LYNNE HUNDLEY

Wind Power

Is it true, Lord?
What your kitchen-monk said
long ago —
Those who have the gale
of the Holy Spirit
go forward
even in sleep —
Is it true?

Then hurl your spirit
like a tempest
into my heart and mind.

Send that same force
which moved
upon the face of the waters

To move upon me —
to create
to cultivate
to propagate —
To move through me
to others

That not only may I run
and not be weary,

But they, too, will exult
in the power
of your restless wind.

WANDA M. TRAWICK

Soaring with the Spirit

WHILE I WAS VISITING in the home of one of our members, a six-year-old boy presented me with a gift: a miniature, hand-made kite. To show my appreciation I began pulling it through the air by its string. The boy quickly announced: "It takes wind for it to fly!"

Life consists of too many obstacles to soar on our own: personal disappointments and difficulties, social tensions and tragedies. To move through life, with all its intrusions and inconveniences, we need God's Spirit — to propel and stabilize, to provide power and strength, to offer purpose and sailing, and to enable peace and satisfaction.

A six-year-old boy reminded me that a kite will not be what it is meant to be without wind. Pentecost teaches us that we will not be who we are meant to be without wind-Spirit.

BOB YOUNTS

Pentecost Sequel

"In a little while," he told them,
"you will see me again."
He did not say how the sight
    would come,
only that it surely would.

They waited;
and the wind came, blowing
    freely.
They waited;
and the fire came, leaping
    joyfully.
They waited;
and the Spirit came, kindly as
    a dove.

The wind kissed their fear
and hurled a fierce hope
    before them.
The fire was a blazing passion,
consuming life within them.
And the dove lifted them
on wings of incomprehensible
    peace and joy.

Then, consumed by their
    coming,
they went
and consumed the world with
    Christ's love.
And now we come,
waiting.

DANIEL H. EVANS

A Confession while Waiting

I wait behind the library desk,
Patiently checking out books,
Usually strange books:
Who would want to read that?
I wait, hoping that, someday,
Someone will put on the desk the very stack of books
I myself would choose.
I wait for that kindred spirit,
That person just like me.
I fantasize about a friendship, even a marriage,
With such a person,
One with whom I would have nearly everything
    in common.
Wouldn't that be perfect?

I seek a community of clones.
How often have I looked for a church, a job, an
    organization
Filled with people just like me?
Wake me up, Lord, to Pentecost.
Let me be willing to find community with those whose
    books may even be written in a different language.

KATHY K. GROW

Come, Holy Spirit, Come!

ALL: Pentecost —

LEFT: when the Spirit blows the dust from our old ways of being the church

RIGHT: and reveals something new and exciting.

ALL: Pentecost —

LEFT: when the Spirit shakes the layers of apathy from our lives

RIGHT: and rebuilds us as bold witnesses and ardent disciples.

ALL: Pentecost —

LEFT: when the Spirit burns away all the hate and hostility within our hearts

RIGHT: and rekindles within us hearts of charity and goodwill.

ALL: Pentecost —

LEFT: when the Spirit melts away the walls that divide

RIGHT: and restores unity among every sister and brother in every land,

ALL: Pentecost —

LEFT: when the Spirit cleanses the tainted and tarnished parts of our past

RIGHT: and redeems us for a good and glorious future.

ALL: Pentecost —

LEFT: when the Spirit touches our tired bodies and weary minds

RIGHT: and revives us with empowered perspective.

ALL: Pentecost —

LEFT: when the Spirit lifts from our lives those attitudes of revenge and feelings of superiority

RIGHT: and replaces them with reconciliation and equality.

ALL: Pentecost —

LEFT: when the Spirit breathes upon our critical and complaining ways

RIGHT: and replenishes our souls with songs of joy and praise.

ALL: Pentecost —

LEFT: when the Spirit comes!

RIGHT: Come, Holy Spirit, come!

ALL: Come, Holy Spirit, come!

BOB YOUNTS

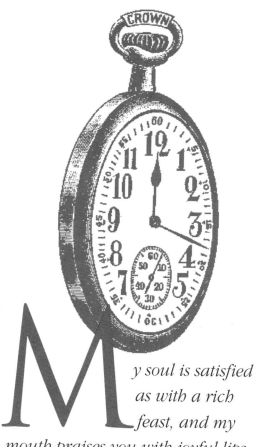

GOD,

MY HELP,

REMIND ME

THAT EVEN IN MY

ORDINARY LIFE

I ALWAYS DWELL

IN THE SHADOW

OF YOUR

EXTRAORDINARY

WINGS.

LET ME SING

FOR JOY!

Amen

My soul is satisfied as with a rich feast, and my mouth praises you with joyful lips when I think of you on my bed, and meditate on you in the watches of the night; for you have been my help, and in the shadow of your wings I sing for joy.

PSALM 63:5-7

Ordinary Time

THERE IS A SEASON WHICH the church has traditionally named Ordinary Time. Commonly we
call it Pentecost, though that isn't technically cor-
rect, since the Sundays in this season are Sundays
after Pentecost rather than Sundays in Pentecost.
Ordinary Time seems a more appropriate name.
This is the season that stretches from the end of
May until the end of November, the season
through which we plod in our ordinary, common
way, enduring the summer heat and the lack of
any high and holy days. Lent and Easter are
behind us. Advent and Christmas are far away.

Yet on some days I suspect that the ordinary
ground I walk on during this season holds mys-
teries beneath it. Occasionally they are uncov-
ered, excavated by joy or by pain. Often I only
sense they are there, silent and very old, under-
girding the commonness and routine of my life,
ancient wisdom in which I am grounded. And I
am moved to take off my shoes, and dance on
the holy ground that is my ordinary life, and
yours.

SUSAN ROSS

The Daily
Is the
Measure

THE DAILY IS THE measure of a number of things. The daily measures our fidelity. The daily measures our responsibility. Dailiness is the measure of love. Dailiness is the measure of the God of surprises.

It's only in the daily that we can leave room for the extraordinary.

JOAN CHITTISTER, OSB

Monday Morning

You served breakfast
on the beach,
broke bread with thousands
at a hillside picnic,
celebrated
at the marriage in Cana.
Exciting events —
all of these.

But this morning
it's only me,
on an ordinary Monday
requesting the honor
of your presence
at my kitchen table
for coffee and conversation.
Comfort comes in knowing
you require neither
feasts nor crowds —
only an invitation.

JOAN RAE MILLS

Sabbath of Location

THERE ARE PLACES that are holy to me, and to other people they might not mean that much — a patch of my own backyard where, the summer after we moved, I would go out after a busy day and after the heat had gone and sit in the darkness and listen to the cicadas and watch the branches of trees move against the starry sky. There's one streetlight I can see from out there, and when I sit on my favorite chair the light comes between two curving arcs of tree branches and it's like two hands, holding the light between them. The same place in the early morning is fresh and cool, and holy, too, but a different place.

There are other places — a bed of lilies of the valley that ran along the north side of the house I grew up in, a small forest beside a river bank where our family used to go when we were all younger.

Someone has spoken of "the sabbath of location," and I guess that describes what these places are to me.

I go to them, and it's like stepping into a different world. I go, and I listen, and I feel the air on my face, and I look, really look, at that world, and something comes to me — a sense of belonging to the universe, the memory of all the love I've been

⊰ What places are holy to you?

⊰ How do you feel when you are in those places?

⊰ What keeps you from staying longer there?

surrounded with in my life, some energy and direction from the peace and loveliness and history of that place — and from myself.

The God in me. The God out there. I breathe it all in through my skin, and I'm a better person.

There's a danger that I could stay too long. But more danger — at least so far — that I won't stay long enough.

MARTHA WHITMORE HICKMAN

SUGGESTED SCRIPTURE READINGS:
Exodus 3:1-12
Exodus 16
1 Kings 19:1-18
Psalm 139:1-18
Matthew 13:31-33
Luke 10:38-42

Stilled Time

Common days, drowsed in
   summer,
One like another,
Morning dew in grasses,
Noontime tea in glasses
   Perspiring icily.
Life clinging close,
A cotton shirt soaked through.
Stilled time,
Stalled.

Time to ponder
   a broken shoelace,
Tying a square knot
   with old childhood skill.
Wondering if a strained, near-
broken friendship
   Can be knotted too.
Working it through.

Turning to God, listening
Beside still waters
In a green pasture.

Mending time.
Spirit time.
Healing,
On a sultry, ordinary day.

HOWARD H. REMALY

As Often as You Eat

I DON'T QUITE REMEMBER when it happened, but suddenly eating a simple meal was never the same. The Words of Institution, which I'd learned as a child, shimmered with new meaning: "Do this in remembrance of me; do this as oft as ye drink. . . ."

What would happen, I wondered, if I experienced not only the ritual meal of Eucharist as holy but every meal as holy? What might it mean for each meal to be a "remembrance" of Christ? Remembrance has its roots in the Latin, meaning "to be mindful of again." What if, as I filled my body with food, I also filled my mind and heart with the fullness of Christ — the power, compassion, healing, forgiveness, affirmation of life that he lived each day?

Each meal we eat is a miracle — a sign of regeneration, of life overcoming death, of seed falling to earth so that new life might emerge. Each meal is a gift that grows more sacred as we recognize with wonder the planting and harvest, the intertwining of our lives with and our dependence on the earth and its bounty, the joining of our hearts with those with whom we break bread — and those with whom we do not; all connects us with the holy. Each meal we eat is a reminder of that. Here, in this very ordinary act, we are invited to receive holy sustenance that we may become as Christ, a "remembrance" of Christ in the world.

The fellowship of the meal — the colorful cornucopia of fruits, grains, and vegetables; the care-

ful preparation of food and table; the gathering of friends, loved ones, and strangers — reminds us of the life and vitality of Christ. Even hurried meals in the midst of harried days can, through a moment of mindfulness and grace, draw us into remembrance, celebration, and thanksgiving. Each time we share a meal with others or savor a quiet meal by ourselves, we participate in a sacred mystery. Just as we are sustained physically by the food we eat, we are also sustained spiritually, moment by moment, as often as we eat, as often as we drink.

JEAN M. BLOMQUIST

A Living Benediction

When the day is too busy and the voices too loud,
    When there is too much on my mind and too little in my heart,
    When I plan too much for tomorrow
        and explain too much about yesterday,
    When faith is a Sunday word
        and "Let's be practical" my motto through the week,
    When I have hidden my true feelings inside
        and then been tempted to complain of being lonely
        and misunderstood,
    When I am quite hopelessly lost
        and don't even have sense enough to know it,
Be my good shepherd and my friend.
Gather up my jangled nerves,
My tensed muscles,
My anxious and fluttering heart.
    Gather up my fearful heart and hold it warmly in your hand;
    Warm it with your spirit and set it glowing.
    Send life pulsing through it like an irresistible flood;
    Quicken me to a quivering blaze,
    Excited and alive!
But show me how to be quiet too, please.
Teach me to be still as the forest pool;
In the deep stillness let me rest.
Let silence surround me like a friend,
Calming me and instructing me
With your wisdom from within.
    When my day is too busy and the voices are all too loud,
    Be my good shepherd and my friend.
    Through fire and water let me be blessed
    That I may be your living benediction
        in the world. Amen.

GEORGE L. MILLER

Beauty That Heals

Could it be that my willingness to feel the pain of my friend
whose seventeen-year-old son has never known his father
and weeps for him these days,
if carried willingly, brings strength to me?

Could it be that to see the leaves of my elm tree,
once green with the vigor of youth,
and now glowing in a lifeless golden banquet,
gives power afresh to my weary soul?

Could it be that to know that my parent,
absent in flesh for a score and two years,
now holds my tender heart each day and invites me, in spirit,
to live past the dawn?

Could it be that to hear a doctor's news of my broken body
is an invitation to trust anew
in the Recreator's constant Covenant promise?

Could it be that my awareness and agony of the hungry children,
the unfairly paid workers, the arrogant ruler,
is an invitation for my faithful stance
for justice to roll down like a mighty stream?

What appears to be desert, scorching sands,
is really, if given proper attention,
the beauty that heals my worn and weary and depleted soul.

Suffering, death, absence, and pain are linked
in a wreath of beauty that heals.

PHYLLIS TYLER-WAYMAN

Barefooted

THE DAY HAD BEGUN just as so many others. Moses rolled off his hard pallet, put on his sandals, shook the sand off his robes, drank a cup of warm tea with goat's milk, and once more went out to check on the herds of his father-in-law.

There were a few clouds in the skies, the wind was still, and no sounds entered his ears. There was nothing particularly special about this day; it was just another lonely, uneventful piece of time to endure. Moses kicked over a rock, watched a lizard scurry for a new respite from the sun, sidestepped a leaving from where a sheep had been, and gazed into the horizon.

Then, almost from nowhere a bush appeared — a bush like so many others under which he had napped. But this one was different; it was on fire. There was a flame, but there was no smoke and no ashes.

Moses was paralyzed. He did not know whether to run or wait to see what happened.

The decision was made for him. Just as he turned for closer investigation, he heard a voice.

"Moses, it's me, God. Now take off your shoes because you are standing on holy ground."

God wanted Moses to get the full effect of what it was like to be in his presence. He did not want Moses insulated from creation.

God wanted the earth to speak to him, to say to him, "Moses, this world belongs to the Creator God. Feel it; let it seep into your toes. How can you dance when you don't feel the ground beneath you? And when the Lord talks to you, you know you are going to dance."

DARRIS K. DOYAL

Y*ou shall love the Lord you God with all your heart, and with all your soul, and with all your strength, and with all your mind; and your neighbor as yourself.*

LUKE 10:27

GENEROUS GOD, YOU ANOINT ME WITH A LAVISH LOVE. HELP ME POUR OUT MY GIFTS, OFFERING THEM TO YOUR SERVICE WITH ALL MY HEART, SOUL, STRENGTH, AND MIND.

Amen

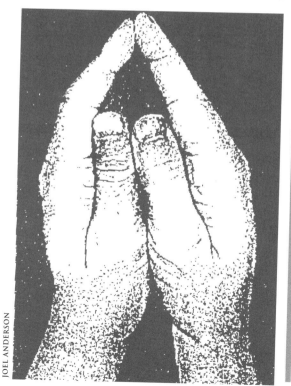

JOEL ANDERSON

Shoes and Socks

OUR WEDNESDAY NIGHT BIBLE study group has become a rather odd community of sorts. We gather about 5:15 p.m. and share whatever food people have been able to bring. While we eat, we share joys and sorrows, celebrations and concerns, and all the stuff that falls in between. There are usually six to ten of us — two or three people who are struggling with mental health problems, three men who are homeless, several dealing with time in prison, and others wrestling with emotional and physical scars. Folks come with a hunger for healing, wanting food for the body and soul, and a place to be at home.

After eating, we take turns reading one or two of the lectionary passages and sharing whatever comes to mind as we try to discern words of challenge and comfort, words that might feed us anew.

John, one of the men who is currently homeless and staying, as the others who are homeless do, at the downtown mission, started out one night: "I got to tell a story on my own self. Happened this morning. See, I been trying so hard to live this new life. To stay clean. I just am really trying, for the first time, to live this stuff out. Some of you don't know how I used to live — drinking, drugging, knocking folks around. I always did read the Bible but I just did it to put other folks down —

quote stuff I wanted and go on about my business. It didn't mean nothing then. But it do now. And it's hard. It really is hard to live this stuff out. And sometimes it seems the more I try the harder it gets.

"Stayed down at the mission again last night — house of pain for real. Woke up this morning and my shoes were gone. Somebody stole my shoes. I didn't even have to think about what to do — I pulled out my knife and I went looking. I was walking all up and down the dining hall, table by table, and I meant to get my shoes back. Kept thinking: in the old days

wouldn't anybody tried to touch my shoes — cause they'd know I'd get 'em 'fore they could ever put 'em on. Oh yeah. I was mean and folks knew it. Didn't care. And that's how it was this morning. It's one thing to give up drinking and drugging. It's another thing when they steal your shoes.

"And I'm hollering, threatening, and walking up and down with my knife out where everyone can see. I'm going to get my shoes. Then old Jim here (points to another homeless man in the group) starts hollering from the other side of the room: 'Bible says if they take one cloak, give

⇨ *Like John in the story, sometimes it is hard to live out our faith.*

⇨ *For you what would be the equivalent of giving up your socks?*

⇨ *What's the hardest part of living out your faith?*

⇨ *What would it mean in your actions for you to walk with Jesus daily?*

⇨ *Choose and carry out an action of faith that is hard for you. Before and after the activity, read Luke 18:31 and pray, dedicating your activity to God.*

SUGGESTED SCRIPTURE READINGS:

Esther 4
Jeremiah 1:4-19
Matthew 5:17-30
Matthew 6:19-21, 25-34
Romans 4:1-5, 13-17
2 Corinthians 5:20b-6:10

them your other one; if they took your shoes, give 'em your socks. Put that knife away and give 'em your socks.'

"And I'm swearing and getting madder. Ain't giving nobody nothin'! I want my shoes! And old Jim, he just keeps hollering: 'Give em your socks, John!'

"Folded up my knife. Took a long time doing it, too. Walked barefoot to the service center this morning — and got me some more shoes — but damned if it ain't hard to live this stuff out!"

JANET WOLF

Waves

AS I SAT ON THE shore of the ocean, I thought of life and the people who have been my friends, and perhaps more important, the people who have refused to be my friends . . . and a wave rolled in with careless beauty and grace, the white foam reaching out to meet me. Slowly it pulled back, by a force greater than its own, into the sea.

I thought of Jesus who will always be there — ready to listen and smile and let me know he loves me, infinitely more than I deserve . . . and a wave rolled in everchanging. The white salty fringe came toward me joyously, loudly, rolling and jumping, and slowly it was pulled back, by a force greater than its own, into the sea.

I thought of myself and people I had to hurt, and help, and love, and cry with in order to remain myself . . . and a wave rolled in making a loud crash. Slowly, silently, the white fringe reached out for me, and slowly was pulled back, by a force greater than its own, into the sea.

I thought of people who took me in — into their hearts, their minds, and their souls — the people who trusted me. Trust, I thought to myself, is one of the greatest forms of love . . . and the wave came again, the white fringe stretching by, not able to touch me. Slowly a force greater than its own pulled it back into the sea.

I thought of how closed I was. I realized in order to find out how to live, I must reach back, especially when reached for — and the wave came back, majestic and powerful. The white fringe reached for me, and I reached out for it. I came closer and closer to the fringe, noticing the light soft texture of it. And so I went forth, past the fringe, into the heart of the wave. Slowly a force greater than my own pulled me into the sea . . . and I died . . . and I lived . . . and I died . . . and I lived . . . and in the process, I learned how to swim.

DIANE L. WILSON

To Lead as I Am?

When I turn to you, Lord,
    you ask me to
    Go, and Do!
How can I
    when I am
    without your loving touch?

In my giftedness,
    use me.
In my hesitancy,
    encourage me.
In my successes,
    humble me.
In my weakness,
    strengthen me.
In my foolishness,
    forgive me.

In my failures,
    direct me.
In my dreaming,
    fulfill me.
In my emptiness,
    fill me.
In my woundedness,
    heal me.

Lord, help me to be open
    to your surrounding love.
As you send me,
    as I am becoming,
    you can use me
    as I am.

TOM LANE

Breakfast

When they had finished break-fast, Jesus said to Simon Peter, "Simon, son of John, do you love me more than these?" He said to him, "Yes, Lord; you know that I love you." [Jesus] said to him, "Feed my lambs."

JOHN 21:15

MORNING IS NOT a good time for me to engage in serious conversation. I am usually half asleep, grumpy, with a bad taste still in my mouth and a mean outlook on life. I am not fully human until sometime in mid-afternoon, long after lunch. Breakfast is not the time to ask me if I love someone or some-thing, and it is especially not the time to tell me to do something.

But this is precisely what happens to Peter in this passage. And it has happened to me as well. At the most inopportune times, Jesus shows up and expects me to deal with his issues and concerns. He asks troubling and annoying ques-tions, such as "Do you love me?"

And I try to answer. "Sure I do, Lord. Don't I serve you? Am I not in the 'Jesus business'? Didn't I give up so much just to be a follower of you? I could have been a somebody, but I became a minister instead. If that isn't love, then I don't know

Conversation

what is."

Jesus does not buy this. He never does. I protest too much and he knows it. And so Jesus adds the punch line. The one that gets me in the gut. "Feed my lambs," he says.

Just like that. Like I am supposed to just take this statement and make something out of it. I mean, after all, he is the good shepherd — he can feed them himself if they need food. I am too tired, too self-centered, too self-satisfied. This is not my job. I was not called to be a sheep feeder.

But again the question comes, and my reply, and then his. And again. And slowly I become aware of what he is trying to say to me. The guilt comes as I realize I have missed the whole point of what it means to be a follower of Jesus. And like Peter I become distressed and even a little sad. I look up at him and see his face and his hands, and then I reach out to get the feeding bucket he holds. I walk toward the sheep in a very sheepish sort of way, and pray silently that I don't again soon forget what true love requires.

WILL HUMES

Confession

In the confines of my soul

and private thoughts,

in my self-righteous

state of mind,

I give to the hungry,

I'm a friend to all,

eager to do

what others will not.

But in the light of reality

I see soiled streaks

on my clean sweater

where he begged for food

and I pushed him away

because he was dirty

and I thought I was

not.

JANNA BETH PERRY

The Minister

THE TELEPHONE RANG. "She's dying. Grandma is dying," the voice said.

I had known it would come. In and out of a coma in the hospital and then in a nursing home, Grandma Sudley had been dying for months. I had seen her grow less and less at home in her body.

Though I knew the call would come, I had not even gone to find my seminary notes on ministering to the dying. Even if they were there, the pages would be blank for me. I knew they would not help.

It's a long way from the parking lot at the hospital to the second room down from the waiting room on the third floor — but not nearly far enough. I was trying to think what in the world someone says to a friend who is dying.

Dying. My God! The thought made my neck crawl. Suppose she just lies there and dies. What do I do? What will I say to the family? Or worse, suppose she does not die, and I have to spend hour after hour with her, trying to say something comforting.

My problem was not that I did not know her. Grandma and I had spent a lot of time together. I used to go over to see her when I wanted to say that I was making shut-in calls but did not really want to go through the agony of listening again to how someone's spouse died or hearing about the aches and pains that the years often bring. When I just wanted to visit a friend, I would go to see Grandma Sudley.

"How are all the old ladies?" she would say.

"They're still after me," I would say.

"Not me," she would say.

"Not me. I've had enough of getting breakfast for some lazy man. Me? I'll take my independence and the peace and quiet of a good night's sleep."

She would ask me to say a prayer with her just so I would feel like I was doing my job, even though both of us knew she prayed oftener and better than I ever thought of.

Now she was dying.

I prayed my way through the front foyer and up the stairs.

Her family was there in a little expectant clutch. Her daughter and son-in-law and her son and daughter-in-law and some assorted cousins — they all looked like they are supposed to look — hurt and frightened.

"I came as fast as I could," I said.

They all stood there and looked at me. They thought I knew what to do.

"Has the doctor been in?" I asked.

"Yes," they said. And still they stared at me, waiting for me to do my pastoral things — whatever I did when people were dying.

"How is she feeling?" I asked to fill the silence, and immediately I wished I could take the question back.

"The doctor said she's dying," her son said.

"That's too bad," I said.

The silence roared in my ears.

"I think she is ready," her daughter said. "She has been praying."

I knew she would be.

The nurse came out of the room. "Reverend," she said. "You can go in for a while now. I think she would like to see you."

"Me?" I said.

The nurse looked around. "You are her pastor?"

"Yes, but only for a short while. I've only been here for a few months." I guess I thought someone might show up who might be in a better position to minister to Grandma.

"You can go in if you want to," the nurse repeated.

"I'll wait until the family has seen her," I volunteered.

"We've been there," they said.

"I guess I'll go in," I said.

"Yes," they said.

Grandma looked so tired. She was breathing hard. They had a tube in her nose and some other tubes in her arms. They were dripping.

"God help me." It was the

best prayer I could think of. I stood there for a while hoping that she would not wake up. Then she opened her eyes and saw me. She smiled.

"How are all your old ladies?" she said in a whisper.

"Still trying to get me." I tried to smile, too.

"Not me," she said.

There was a silence for a long time. I held her hand. It was hard and soft and brittle. After a while she looked at me again.

"I guess I'm going to leave," she said.

"I know," I said.

"I'm very tired."

"I know," I said again.

"I never died before," she smiled again a little bit.

"I've never been with someone who died before," I said.

"I think we'll make it, Pastor." She was almost whispering. She squeezed my hand a little.

"Will you listen while I pray?" Her eyes were closed. I did not answer. She knew what I would say.

"My Father," she whispered, "take me home because of my Jesus. And Father, take care of this good boy here. He has given love, and he has been my friend. Amen."

I was crying. "Thank you, Grandma," I said.

"It's all right. I'm just going to be with a friend. Tell them out there that I'm all right."

"I'll tell them, Grandma," I said.

She closed her eyes and fell asleep. I never saw her alive again. I told her family what she told me to say. They thought I was a wonderful and comforting minister. I never told them that Grandma had told me what to say.

Sometimes when I drive by the little cemetery along the country road where we buried her, I stop — even if it is a hot day and I am in a hurry — and I think about her for a while. And I say a prayer — a prayer she could have said so much better than I — and thank God for that great woman who knew so well how to minister to me. I look at her grave across the hill by the tree. "We made it, Grandma," I say. "We made it."

TED SCHROEDER

Come to [Christ], a living stone, though rejected by mortals yet chosen and precious in God's sight, and like living stones, let your lives be built into a spiritual house.

1 PETER 2:4-5

LOVING GOD,
WE LONG
FOR COMMUNITY.
MAKE US
LIVING STONES
THROUGH CHRIST.
BOND US INTO
A SPIRITUAL HOUSE.
MAKE OUR
DWELLING PLACE
SECURE.

Amen

A Lighted Procession

SEVERAL YEARS AGO I participated in a training
event for youth workers. One night our worship
included climbing up on top of a canyon wall
and spending time looking at the stars. We
listened to the words of the first chapter of
Genesis, punctuated by the sounds of nighttime
creation and by the cries of a two-month-old
baby who was part of our group. We heard
words about light — the light with which God
graces us and the light we give to one another.
And then each of us was given a candle, and we
lit them and walked single file down the path
back to the canyon.

We were silent as we walked. Occasionally
someone began a song or spoke words to someone near them, often words of guidance: "Watch
out for that rock," or "There's a big step down
here." But mostly we were silent.

There was a breeze blowing across the top of
the canyon that night, and sometimes it caught a
candle flame and extinguished it. But the bearer
of that candle was always cared for by the one
walking in front or behind; the candle was relit,
and the procession continued.

I was walking near the front of the line. As we
wound down the path, I looked back and up the
side of the canyon and saw sixty or seventy lights
like my own, flickering at times, going out, being

The Courage to Be

Read Luke 10:25-37

When what we call our faith
discourages or prevents
our showing love to others
we had better stop
and listen and look
and recognize
how very much
easier it is
to be the priest or levite
than to summon
the courage to be
the neighbor.

THOMAS JOHN CARLISLE

rekindled; but always moving, slowly, carefully, in quiet and awesome beauty.

In my office there is a plaque, given to me by a friend, with these words by Albert Schweitzer: *Sometimes our light goes out but is blown again into flame by an encounter with another human being. Each of us owes the deepest thanks to those who have rekindled this inner light.*

We are those who move in a procession, a march through the darkness. The lights we carry are much alike, though each is individually our own. And when they are blown out in spite of our efforts to protect them from sudden winds, we need each other in order to continue the procession, to see the way ahead. So we move on, our flickering light joining other lights in a communion — in a community — that is indeed awesome and beautiful.

SUSAN ROSS

An Exaltation of Fellowship

I'VE NEVER SEEN A LARK. I've seen lots of red-winged blackbirds and my fair share of robins and sparrows. A cardinal chose to spend one winter in my backyard, as did a blue jay once; but I've never seen a lark.

I'd like to. Actually, I don't think one would be enough. I'd have to see ten, or thirty, or however many it takes for them to warrant their proper group name: an exaltation.

I think I can imagine what they would be like. They'd swoop through the air, flutter from tree to tree, trill out of pure joy, sing their excitement over this day, this hour, this moment.

People, I've noticed, are never referred to as an exaltation. When we group together, we're called a committee, or a circle, or a congregation, or an assembly. Very rarely do we deserve a more special name.

A few times though (I can count them on my fingers), I've been part of an exaltation.

Just before Christmas last year, a very friendly baby was baptized in our church. Halfway through the ritual, she noticed the minister's left ear. She touched it with an inquiring finger. She tweaked it. She yanked it. She wiggled it. All the while, she smiled at it. We in the congregation smiled too — at her, and at each other. For a moment, we were an exaltation.

Recently my friend Beth announced at choir practice that she'll be leaving us soon: she's been called and is on her way to seminary. All of us — sopranos, altos, basses, and tenors — threw our arms around her, pumped her hand, chorused our pleasure. We were an exaltation.

Those moments can't be engineered, constructed, or requisitioned. They come in their own time, usually without advance warning or sign. We cannot know when to expect them or how to find them. All we can do is recognize their arrival and rejoice.

When those moments come, we find that a shared sense of joy and well-being has united a group of individuals. We have become an exaltation — an expression of joy.

MARY CARTLEDGE-HAYES

A Story of Peace

LET ME TELL YOU a story of world peace — a story of the stuff of world community.

The main character in this story is six years old. His name is Hermon (like the name of the mountain in the Bible) and he was born in the remote western mountains of Iran, among a people who call themselves Kurdish because once there was a country known as Kurdistan.

The life of Hermon and all the members of his family (parents and three brothers and sister) were threatened by those who had been their ancient enemies both for political and religious reasons, and so they lived in frustration and fear high on a mountain ridge in a tent with other refugees like themselves.

Hermon was born with a cleft lip and a cleft palate and there has never, of course, been any chance to have that corrected. He also suffers a hernia.

Hermon and his Muslim family were selected by a refugee settlement group to be sent to Nashville, Tennessee. Quite by chance, Hermon and his family were assigned to our church, which was asked only twenty-four hours before Hermon arrived if it could take care of this family, find a home for them, feed them, and give them essential provisions.

Members of the church brought clothing to them, shopped for them, made beds for them, gave furniture to them. At last they had their own apartment.

Bob became their advocate, their driver, their manager, their American father. Hoyt and Elizabeth gave a job to Hermon's father; Don took him to his job and showed him how to get home on his own; Roger took Hermon and his brothers and sister to play in the park.

Kathleen taught Hermon's mother how to shop in American supermarkets and how to accomplish simple tasks in her home. Arville provided medical care for Hermon's baby sister, Jiman.

One Friday, Hermon was admitted to the hospital according to some special arrangement made by Luke. Rueben, a plastic surgeon, repaired Hermon's mouth and Whit, a pediatric surgeon, repaired his hernia — all in one surgical session. Nancy took Hermon and his mother to the hospital and sat with his mother through the surgery.

Do you understand what was happening?

God wishes us health and community and world peace, but there was no way to get any of that done unless there was, is, a community of persons willing to let those dreams become reality. We are necessary partners in the enterprise of establishing the kingdom of God in this world.

RUSSELL T. MONTFORT

NINE REFLECTION

☞ *In Luke 10:25-37, Jesus interprets the commandment to love our neighbors to include people who are strangers to us.*

☞ *What do you feel when you hear this instruction from Jesus?*

☞ *What does it mean in your daily life to love even neighbors who are strangers? in the life of your faith community?*

☞ *Think of a time when you were a stranger. How were you welcomed by others?*

SUGGESTED SCRIPTURE READINGS:

Psalm 133

Matthew 4:18-22

Acts 2:43-47

Romans 1:1-12

1 John 1:1-7

Jude 20-25

The Great Baptism

"CAN YOU BAPTIZE him this Sunday?" asked Mrs. Fitzgerald (The Mrs. Fitzgerald whose grandfather founded St. Paul's and whose daughter-in-law had recently given birth to James Walter Fitzgerald III).

"Of course," replied the humble assistant rector (the rector was on vacation and it was an honor to baptize J. W. Fitzgerald III).

Within the context of the 11:00 a.m. service the great baptism began. It was a gala affair. Patriarchs were present in dark suits, matriarchs stood in flowered dresses crowned with broad-brimmed hats. Children looked on in spanking new outfits. The occasion was crowned with dignity only the Fitzgerald family could muster.

The assistant rector did not know how his young son managed to push the button or where he got the money; but the youngster faded out of the congregation into the hallway where he plunked his coins into the big red machine, punched the button, and emerged into the church with a large soda in his grip. The assistant rector did not notice his son working his way up to the edge of the font, nor did he take cognizance of the lad shaking the object he was holding with both hands up and down, up and down. The assistant rector did not guess that his son was about to remove his thumb from the neck of the container.

He did know it when the thumb was clear of the bottle

and the brown sticky liquid came shooting forth. It was right after "suffer the little children to come unto me" that he had to wipe his eyes and prayer book.

The Fitzgeralds are nice people, all of them, nice people. That is why the assistant rector is still the assistant rector. That is also why everyone present that morning grew a bit in their understanding of Christian baptism. Accepting children into the church does not mean simply standing in a nice outfit on a sunny morning in a beautiful building and saying you will love them. It also means loving them when they spray soda all over you.

BENJAMIN H. SKYLES

Splinters

We talked about children and grandchildren, their pictures plastered on the walls like an old time art gallery. The pictures of her sons were from their high school graduations years ago — pink little faces grinning behind stringy tassels. Looking at them, she mused out loud, "It's silly to keep those old pictures up there like that, but that's how I remember them."

In the corner sat a guitar and I couldn't help asking about it. Was she the musician in the family? No, she wasn't, and she laughed at the very suggestion. The guitar had belonged to her husband.

She asked if I played and I answered yes. The instrument was passed awkwardly to me, like it might break at any moment, shatter in the changing of hands.

"Oh, good, you can tune it." Just the thought it was tuned mattered somehow, whether it would be played or not. But I did play. I played one familiar carol after another until she looked me in the eye and said, "Hearing that makes me want to smash it into a pile of splinters."

I stopped.

"He could leave me in a moment with that thing," she said. "The minute it sat in his lap and his fingers touched those strings, his eyes closed, and I was gone. It's how he got away. Not from me in particular, but from everything. And now he is really gone. And I hear those sounds and he's closed his eyes again. But this time for good. He really left. He really got away. And I could smash it to splinters."

Her face made me realize that it was her heart that was in splinters. She just wanted to make the guitar match.

"It reminds me of how I wasn't with him when he died. He was there in the nursing home, but I was sick and just couldn't be there all the time. And I wasn't. I just wasn't there."

I took the guitar and started to return it to its place in the corner. She stopped me with a motion of her hand.

"No," she said, "play that thing some more. Play."

TIM CARSON

Resurrection

God,
sometimes
we're as tightly bound
as Lazarus
in a tomb:
unseeing,
unfeeling,
unmoving.
Then,
in our bondage
you send
another
to help free us;
a friend
who believes
and rolls the stone away.
Unbound,
enabled to emerge
from the caves of our making,
our eyes are opened
to see your loving face.
We are released —
Resurrection!

ROBERTA PORTER

God] has told you, O mortal, what is good; and what does the Lord require of you but to do justice, and to love kindness, and to walk humbly with your God?

MICAH 6:8

GOD,

WHO WORKS

FOR JUSTICE

IN THE WORLD,

YOUR PROPHETS

REMIND US THAT

RATHER THAN

BRINGING SACRIFICES

TO THE ALTAR,

THE WORSHIP

YOU DESIRE

IS JUSTICE, KINDNESS,

AND HUMILITY

IN ALL

OUR DEALINGS.

Amen

Invocation for *God's* Justice

O Lord, our God, worship is a strange activity
For us in this, the twentieth century.
We know, only too well, how to analyze,
To criticize, rationalize, finalize.
The secrets of production and consumption,
Of automation, cybernation, organization
Are hidden from us no longer.
We can replace the human heart,
And set a human being on the moon.
There is nothing we cannot control.
Except, it seems, ourselves.
So we come before you,
A people all-sufficient,
Yet somehow lacking,
A race infinitely powerful,
Yet powerless to achieve justice,
Teach us to worship, Lord,
To know your presence,
To seek your forgiveness,
To become open to your power,
The power which is made perfect
In weakness.
And in your power of love,
May we find justice and truth,
peace and life.
Amen.

J. BARRIE SHEPHERD

When the Tables Are *Turned*

ONE OF THE MOST compelling principles of the gospel is the call for social justice. Christ spent his life among the oppressed and the forgotten, and he tells his followers to do so as well. For a long time, I was removed from this kind of human suffering, though its existence angered me. I could understand its consequences on an intellectual level, but prejudice and poverty remained abstract for me. Eventually I knew I had to do more for people.

Scanning the classifieds one Sunday, I saw an ad for a staff opening at Reconciliation Ministries, an organization that supports families of prison inmates. I got the job and with it came great insight into many social problems. Sometimes the burdens these families carry amaze me — the financial hardships, the ostracism by an angry public, the loneliness of having a loved one in prison. I've learned that people are resilient and that everyone has some capacity to improve the lives of others. There is so much richness of experience in the folks I meet as clients, volunteers, and supporters. All are dedicated to remembering the families of the incarcerated, whom Reconciliation considers the forgotten victims of crime.

I recently received a profound lesson in the effects of victimization. A man entered Reconciliation's open office door and pulled out a gun. My heart and my breathing simply stopped when I saw the weapon. I was totally consumed with fear. It was impossible for me to think. My colleague and I later said that neither of us ever sensed that he would shoot us, but that intuition could not ease my terror at the time. I remember wondering how badly gunshot wounds hurt. After a brief eternity, he took our money and escaped in my co-worker's car.

Several clients asked if I would quit because of the robbery. Their doubts really surprised me since I could not see the connection between what had happened to me and their situations. I finally realized they were afraid I would blame them for the crime. Maybe they were used to receiving blame for the actions of others. I had to reas-sure clients that I would not leave Reconciliation.

My commitment to my work did not diminish after the robbery; in fact, it has strengthened my resolve. Once I dealt with the initial shock, I tried to understand what would motivate someone to risk killing two people in a church basement office for less than $50. My conclusions only intensify my commitment to work for justice.

MARY WILDER

Teach Me

Lord, I am torn by the pain of the world:
Hungry pain from bloated stomachs and matchstick limbs;
Hollow pain from lonely lives in narrow houses;
Searing pain from struggling souls and roiling spirits;
Dull pain from malnourished bodies and hopeless minds;
Tortured pain from heaving chests and twisted torsos;
Aching pain from bitter marriages and blocked communication.
The world is torn, Lord, and I am torn with it.

What do you want me to do?
Show me where to mend, where to love.
Teach me how to mend, how to love.
I cry in my soul: Teach me, teach me to love!

LINDA FELVER

An Affirmation

We are unique human beings linked with all of creation
 and gathered from diverse places
to share a ministry faithfully,
to raise questions hopefully,
to work for justice lovingly.

In whom and in what do we believe?

We believe in God,
 eternal yet ever-moving one,
who creates and is creating,
who keeps covenant with humankind,
who sets before us the ways of life
 and of death.

We believe in Jesus, the servant-advocate,
who lived the way of dying/rising,
who embodied justice and reconciliation,
who, with authority, calls us to share
 this way and this embodying.

We believe in the Holy Spirit, sustaining presence and
 transforming power,
who dwells among us in clarity and in mystery,

who inspires us individually and corporately,
who challenges, prods, emboldens.

We believe in the church, community of faith and caring,
    covenant and promise,
which nurtures our pilgrimage and
through which we are called to be witnesses to
    God's truth, love, and justice.

We believe our believing affects
    our daily walking and talking,
    our doubting and struggling,
    our decisions and choice-making,
    our responses to persons and systems.

We intend in this community in these days
to raise questions hopefully,
to work for justice lovingly,
to share a ministry faithfully,
    and, by God's grace, passionately!

BARBARA B. TROXELL

Feed My Lambs

We look
and never see
the face of hunger
for our eyes are not open.

We listen
and do not hear
the cry of despair
for our ears are stopped up.

We touch
and feel nothing
of the pain of loneliness
for our hearts are grown dull.

In our closed hands
five loaves and two fish
will never be more
than five loaves and two fish.

MARY KULBERG

Read Luke 9:10-17.

Imagine that Jesus has just taken you and other members of your faith community away to a quiet place, but a crowd follows and will not leave you alone.

☞ *Who is in the crowd?*

☞ *What do the people in the crowd need?*

Jesus tells you to feed the crowd.

☞ *How do you react?*

☞ *What do you give the crowd?*

☞ *How might God act in this situation to ensure that all are fed?*

☞ *After the meal, what is left over? What do you collect in the baskets?*

SUGGESTED SCRIPTURE READINGS:

Deuteronomy 24:19-22

Isaiah 61:1-4, 8-11

Amos 2:6-11

Matthew 5:1-12

Matthew 25:31-46

God Has Joined *Reconciliation & Justice*

God has joined reconciliation and justice together, and we dare not put them asunder. Reconciliation without justice is sentimentality. Justice without reconciliation can turn into cruel retribution. We must never be seduced by the heresy of the half gospel.

PETER STOREY

A Prayer
for
Peace &
Reconciliation

PERSISTENT GOD, gather us
around the common table,
where the poor are included,
the peacemakers are renewed,
and the faithful sent to weave
songs of peace and deeds of
justice. Holy God, turn our face
toward kindness, fill our hearts
with your compassion, and
guide our feet along the paths
of peace. For you are the Holy
One who brings the dawn after
the darkest hour and the Freeing
One who desires liberation for
all the oppressed. Work your
will and your way in and
through us for the sake of your
creation. Amen.

LARRY JAMES PEACOCK

Y*ou shall go out in joy, and be led back in peace; the mountains and the hills before you shall burst into song, and all the trees of the field shall clap their hands.*

ISAIAH 55:12

WONDROUS GOD,
CREATOR OF ALL
THAT IS,
WE PRAISE YOU.
SEND US OUT
INTO THE WORLD
IN JOY
AND LEAD US
IN PEACE
AS WE SING
YOUR PRAISES.

Amen

GUSTAV DORÉ

Holy Laughter

I CAME UP OUT OF THE WATER giggling . . . and I couldn't stop. I was embarrassed half to death.

What would the dozen or so faithful members of the little country church that had raised me — my parents and Sunday school teachers and role models — think of my giggles at such a holy moment?

Standing on the bank of our farm pond, they sang "Amazing Grace."

I giggled.

Unlike my older brother and sisters, I had not been baptized as an infant. At the time I was born, the pastor of our church had suggested to my parents that I instead be dedicated and allowed to make my own decision about baptism when I had come of age.

Fifteen years old, attending confirmation class, I discovered I would need to be baptized before I could be confirmed with the rest of my class that coming Easter.

I was given the options of baptism by sprinkling, pouring, or immersion. Since the other options seemed too babyish to my teenaged self, I chose immersion.

Perhaps it was because I was already somewhat embarrassed that I, a fifteen year old, was having done to me what I had only seen done to infants and children.

Perhaps it was because the farm pond water was unbelievably cold, much colder than the warm spring air led me to expect it would be.

Perhaps it was because I had not been prepared to be pushed under the water three times — once for each person of the Trinity — and, taken by surprise, had swallowed a throat full of water the second time under.

I came up the third time coughing and spitting, and then, giggling. For the longest, most mortifying moments of my fifteen years, I couldn't stop giggling. As soon as I thought I had myself under control, I'd burst out again in giggles. Not until after the hymn had been sung, the benediction said, and refreshments served, could I stop myself.

As quickly as I could, I fled into the farm house supposedly to put on dry clothes but really to hide. My mother finally came to find me and tell me it would be impolite not to join the others outside.

When I was congratulated, I didn't know how to reply.

Then an elderly saint of the church, sensing my embarrassment, I think, took me aside and told me I had received a great gift.

There is a thing, she told me, called holy laughter. She explained, "It is a gift of the

Spirit." My laughter was a sign that my spirit understood that baptism meant that nothing on earth or in heaven or in hell could ever really hurt or harm me. The Holy Spirit had relayed that message to my spirit in my baptism. Your spirit is full of great joy; that's why you laughed, she told me.

At the time, I thought she was just trying to make me feel better. It didn't seem to me that it was the Holy Spirit that made me giggle.

I guess, even today, I still wonder whether my laughter was just some combination of my embarrassment at being fifteen, the shocking coldness of the water, and the surprise of going under the water a second and third time.

But part of me hopes that my spirit did receive a message in my baptism that made me laugh with a joy I couldn't understand at the time — a deep inner knowledge that I could never be separated from the love of the God who had claimed and marked me in my baptism. I wonder if this is why my spirit has sometimes been stronger and steadier during frustrations and troubles than the rest of me wanted to be?

So, I tell myself from time to time, especially when I am tempted by fear or discouragement, remember your baptism . . . and giggle.

DEAN J. SNYDER

When I Talk about
Jesus

When I talk about Jesus,
I'm talking about what God has brought forth
and is still bringing forth in my life:
A new faith that has overcome old fears.
A new hope that drives away despair.
A new light that outshines the darkness.
A new wisdom that overshadows ignorance.
A brand new liberation that puts oppression to rest.
A new wholeness that dissipates sexism, racism, and classism.

When I sing, pray, and dance Jesus,
when I smile and raise my hands,
these are expressions of my willingness
to share what I have and also to invite
God to work through my life.
I present to you my living Jesus,
God's offspring in my consciousness and in my living.
And so it is, and so it is.

J. Brendonly Cunningham

My Call to *Play*

I want the child within me
  to come forth in joy
    to dance with delight
      over the creation
        (God's creation — and mine!)
  and when the dance has begun
    to join hands with
      my thinking self
      my faith self and
      my self that aches
        for hurting humanity

And the whole self will sing the praises of God
  by binding up the wounds of the hurt ones
    by lifting the fallen
    by holding up the arms of hope
      for those in despair
  and by laughing with hilarity and glee
    over life itself.

BARBARA S. MCKEE

Prayer of Thanks

Response: We give thee thanks, O God.

For the aardvark and the ant and all other creatures whose names begin with "A"; for the songs of birds, and honey from bees; for furry cats and swimming crayfish; for dingoes, and dolphins that swim in the sea; for elephants, and eagles who soar above the earth, let us say . . .

For frogs which keep us awake at night with their voices; for giraffes whose necks reach to the sky; for hamsters to pet and hogs who give us food; for insects who inhabit our world, let us say . . .

For jackrabbits racing across the desert; for kangaroos and katydids; for lions, lemmings, and lizards; for the mongoose, and monkeys who often remind us of ourselves, let the people say . . .

For nectarines which nourish us; for the octopus and oyster, gifts of the sea; for people, Lord, because we too are part of your creation, let us say . . .

For quartz which runs our watches; for rabbits, rats, and rainstorms; for snakes which slither in the grass; for trees that give us food and shelter; for the power of uranium, may we use it wisely and safely; let the people say . . .

For vipers and violets; for whales who swim the ocean and worms tunneling beneath the earth; for xerophytes; for yaks, and for yeast which leavens our bread; for the zebras, whose stripes are one place where black and white live peacefully together, we say . . .

Lord, all things in your creation are good. Bless all those parts of the earth which we have not mentioned. Make us faithful stewards of the gifts you have given. For it is in Christ's name we pray. Amen.

Susan Thacker-Gwaltney

❧ *What is the color of your thanksgiving?*

❧ *Draw or paint a picture of all you are thankful for. Or make a list of the things you praise God for in your life.*

❧ *Offer your artwork or list to God as a gift. Express thanks to God for each element.*
Conclude with a time of prayer, using the prayer on page 120.

SUGGESTED SCRIPTURE READINGS:

2 Samuel 6:1-5

Psalm 148

Luke 2:25-38

Luke 17:11-19

2 Corinthians 8:1-15

2 Timothy 1:3-14

The Color of Thanksgiving

Somewhere just between the
    green of summer
And the gray of winter,
Is the color of thanksgiving.

The sun is shining brightly
The air is crisp and cool,
Suggesting autumn.
A few trees are
Sprinkled with gold.
They aren't dying,
    you understand,
They are just permitting God
To do the strange and
    wonderful things
God likes to do with trees.

And when are we willing
    to let God
Do the strange and
    wonderful things
God likes to do with people?

What is the color of our
    thanksgiving?

NORM SHOCKLEY